S0-ARM-379

Working Papers

for use with

Intermediate Accounting

Sixth Edition

Lanny G. Chasteen
Oklahome State University

Richard E. Flaherty
Arizona State University

Melvin C. O'Connor
Michigan State University

Prepared by
Diane Tanner
University of North Florida

**Irwin
McGraw-Hill**

Boston   Burr Ridge, IL   Dubuque, IA   Madison, WI   New York   San Francisco   St. Louis
Bangkok   Bogotá   Caracas   Lisbon   London   Madrid
Mexico City   Milan   New Delhi   Seoul   Singapore   Sydney   Taipei   Toronto

Irwin/McGraw-Hill

A Division of The McGraw·Hill Companies

Working Papers for use with
INTERMEDIATE ACCOUNTING

Copyright ©1998 by The McGraw-Hill Companies, Inc. All rights reserved.
Previous editions 1995 and 1992 by McGraw-Hill, Inc.
Printed in the United States of America.
The contents of, or parts thereof, may be reproduced for use with
INTERMEDIATE ACCOUNTING
Lanny G. Chasteen, Richard E. Flaherty, and Melvin C. O'Connor
provided such reproductions bear copyright notice and may not be reproduced in
any form for any other purpose without permission of the publisher.

1 2 3 4 5 6 7 8 9 0 BKM/BKM 9 0 9 8

ISBN 0-07-292924-3

http://www.mhhe.com

Note to the Student

The *Working Papers* are provided to assist you in preparing answers to homework problems. Selected exercises and problems in *Intermediate Accounting*, Sixth Edition, have an appropriately formatted worksheet that uses both sides of the page, thus minimizing the number of pages that you will need to organize. Many chapters have generic forms at the beginning of the chapter that you may use for assignments with omitted working papers.

Unless you are told otherwise by your accounting teacher, you will want to prepare each working paper in pencil (preferably a No. 2 pencil). Also, you will want to purchase a good eraser because it is inevitable that you will make some mistakes.

When you tear out each page from the *Working Papers*, be sure to crease the page along the perforation before detaching it so that the page tears evenly.

Mastering intermediate accounting is a challenging goal. In order to achieve that goal, you will find that it is necessary to be diligent in preparing homework assignments. These *Working Papers* will assist you in accomplishing your goal.

E2–1

1.	7.
2.	8.
3.	9.
4.	10.
5.	11.
6.	12.

E2–2

1.	10.
2.	11.
3.	12.
4.	13.
5.	14.
6.	15.
7.	16.
8.	17.
9.	18.

E2–7

	1998	1999	2000
1. Cash-basis accounting:			
2. Accrual-basis accounting:			

E2–8 Accrual-basis income:

	1998	1999

E2–9

E2–10

1. Nominal dollars:

2. General purchasing power units at the end of 1998:

3. Physical capital:

E2–11

1. Maintaining capital in nominal dollars:

2. Maintaining capital in units of general purchasing power:

3. Maintaining capital in physical units:

E3–1	Debit	Credit		Debit	Credit
1.			6.		
2.			7.		
3.			8.		
4.			9.		
5.			10.		

E3–2   Note: Not all answers require debits/credits.

	Debit	Credit
1. a)		
b)		
c)		
d)		
e)		

2.

Rebenar Racquet Club

Trial Balance

December 31, 1998

	Debit	Credit

To the Student:

The following few pages contain generic journal entry and financial statement forms that may be used for omitted exercises and problems.

	Debit	Credit

	Debit	Credit

	Debit	Credit

	Debit	Credit

	Debit	Credit

E3–10

1. and 2.

Salaries Expense	Salaries Payable

Income Summary	Cash

3. _____

_____

_____

_____

4.		Debit	Credit

5. _____

_____

E3–11

1. Cost of goods sold:

_____

_____

_____

2. Ending inventory:

_____

_____

_____

3. Purchases:

_____

_____

_____

4. Beginning inventory:

_____

_____

E3–13

Scotty Moore

Balance Sheet

December 31, 1998

Assets		Liabilities and Equity	

E3–19

	Net Income		Total Assets, 12/31		Total Liabilities, 12/31		Operating Cash Flows	
	1997	1998	1997	1998	1997	1998	1997	1998
a)	+ $1,000	+ $3,000	+ $1,000	+ $3,000	$ –0–	$ –0–	$ –0–	+ $1,000
b)								
c)								
d)								
e)								

E3–20

1. a)

   b)

   c)

2.

P3–1 or P3–2

T-accounts

Cash

P3–3 (continued)

1. and 3. cont.

Purchases	Salary Expense

Dividends Payable	Sales Returns

	Debit	Credit

P3–3 (concluded)

5.

TJ's Golf-Around

Income Statement

For the Year Ending December 31, 1998

6.

TJ's Golf-Around

Balance Sheet

December 31, 1998

P3–8 Please see end of book for worksheet.

P3–9

Larry's Plumbing Company

Income Statement

For the Year Ended January 31, 1998

Larry's Plumbing Company

Balance Sheet

January 31, 1998

P3–12

Note: Use the T-accounts below to post transaction entries and adjusting and closing entries for September, and transaction entries and adjusting entries for October.

Cash	Building

	Accumulated Depreciation

	Supplies

Land	

Accounts Receivable	Allowance for Doubtful Accounts

Accounts Payable	Usry, Capital

Sales	Inventory

Purchases	Salary Expense

P3–12 (continued)

Salaries Payable	Depreciation Expense

Supplies Expense	Other Expenses

Income Summary	Uncollectible Accounts Expense

Cost of Goods Sold	

P3–12 (concluded)

Usty Borthers Clothiers

Income Statement

For the Month of October 1998

Usry Bothers Clothiers

Balance Sheet

October 31, 1988

P3–14

Linehan Oil Jobbers

Income Statement

For the Year Ending December 31, 1998

Linehan Oil Jobbers

Balance Sheet

December 31, 1998

P3–15 Please see end of book for worksheet.

P3–16

	Trial Balance		Adjustments		Income Statement		Balance Sheet	
	DR.	CR.	DR.	CR.	DR.	CR.	DR.	CR.
Cash	45						45	
Receivables	70		25				95	
Prepaid insurance				5			10	
Plant and equipment	80						80	
Accumulated depreciation		20						
Accounts payable		40						40
Unearned revenue			20					5
Salaries payable		0						
Common stock		20						
Contributed capital								
in excess of par		20						
Retained earnings		45						
Revenues		100						
Salaries expense			15		40			
Depreciation expense	0				10			
Insurance expense								
Other expenses	35				35			
Total								
Net income (loss)								
Total								

Calculations:

Instructor ________________ Section ________________ Name ________________

E4–1

1.

2.

E4–2

1. Income calculation:

2.

E4–3

1. Income calculation:

2.

E4–4 or E4–5

Income Statement

For the Year Ended December 31, 1998

E4–6 or E4–7

   1. Single-step income statement:

Income Statement

For the Year Ended December 31, 19XX

(in thousands except per share amounts)

E4–6 or E4–7 (concluded)

  2. Multiple-step income statement:

Income Statement

For the Year Ended December 31, 19XX

(in thousands except per share amounts)

  3.

E4–8 or E4–9

Income Statement

For the Year Ended December 31, 1998

E4–10

E4–11

E4–12

LaFrentz Corporation

Partial Income Statement

For the Year Ended December 31, 1998

E4–13

Lorek, Inc.

Partial Income Statement

For the Year Ended December 31, 1998

Income from continuing operations										4	8	4	0	0	0 0

E4–14

Dusenbury, Inc.

Combined Statement of Income and Retained Earnings

For the Year Ended December 31, 1998

E4–15   Primary Financial Statements

	1998	1997	1996	1995
Income before change		2 4 6 0 0 0	2 3 8 0 0 0	2 3 0 0 0 0

Pro forma

Note:

P4–1 or P4–2

Income Statement

For the Year Ended

(in thousands except per share amounts)

P4–3 or P4–4

Income Statement

For the Year Ended December 31, 1998

(in thousands except per share amounts)

P4–5

Aspen Corporation

Income Statements

For the Years Ended December 31, 1997 and 1998

(in thousands)

	1998	1997
Income from continuing operations:		

Calculation of correct income from continuing operations:

Calculation of net gain on disposal of segment:

P4–6 **Amount to Report**

Case 1:   o

                                          $r_1 + r_2$

                                          $e_1 + e_2$

Case 2:   o

                                          $r_1 + r_2$

                                          $e_1 + e_2$

Case 3:   o

                                          $r_1 + r_2$

                                          $e_1 + e_2$

Case 4:   o

                                          $r_1 + r_2$

                                          $e_1 + e_2$

P4–7 **Debit** **Credit**

1.

2. **1998** **1997**

P4–8

1. a)

   b)

   c)

   d)

   e)

2. Calculation of correct income from operations:

Tentative income from operations before taxes									4	2	0	0	0	0	0

P4–8 (concluded)

2. (continued)

Mori Corporation

Income Statement

For the Year Ended December 31, 1998

P4-9

| Tentative income from operations before taxes | 44 | 8 | 5 | 0 | 0 | 0 | 0 | |

Finley Media Corporation

Income Statement

For the Year Ended December 31, 1998

P4–10

1. Income from operations before taxes, unadjusted		6	0	0	0	0	0	

2.

Marie Corporation

Partial Income Statement

For the Year Ended December 31, 1998

P4–11

1.

E5–1 ____ Income taxes payable   ____ Accounts payable

____ Goodwill   ____ Organization costs

____ Bonds payable (due in 8 years)   ____ Premium on common stock

____ Petty cash   ____ Buildings

____ Trade accounts receivable   ____ Bond sinking fund

____ Investment in subsidiary   ____ Cash

____ Accrued wages   ____ Deferred rearrangement costs

____ Patents   ____ Accumulated depreciation

____ Raw materials inventory   ____ Discount on bonds payable

____ Mortgage payable   ____ Land (held for speculative purposes)

____ Preferred stock   ____ Prepaid expenses

E5–2 ____ Long term receivables   ____ Allowance for uncollectible accounts

____ Accumulated amortization   ____ Premium on bonds payable

____ Current maturities of long-term debt   ____ Supplies inventory

____ Notes payable (short-term)   ____ Additional paid-in capital

____ Accrued payroll taxes   ____ Work-in-process inventory

____ Leasehold improvements   ____ Notes receivable (short-term)

____ Retained earnings appropriated for plant expansion   ____ Copyrights

____ Machinery   ____ Unearned revenue (long-term)

____ Donated capital   ____ Inventory

____ Deferred tax liability (long-term)   ____ Short-term investments

---

E5–3

1. ____

2. ____

3. ____

E5–4

a.   f.

b.   g.

c.   h.

d.   i.

e.   j.

E5–5

a)

b)

c)

d)

e)

f)

g)

h)

i)

j)

E5–6

Nix Company

Balance Sheet

As of December 31, 1998

Assets	Liabilities and Stockholders' Equity

E5–7

Olsen Photo, Inc.

Balance Sheet

As of December 31, 1998

Assets	**Liabilities and Stockholders' Equity**

E5–8

	Assets	**Liabilities**	**Stockholders' Equity**
a)			
b)			
c)			
d)			
e)			

E5–9

Ramanan Corporation

Balance Sheet

As of December 31, 1998

(in thousands)

E5–10

1.

2.

	Debit	Credit

E5–14

1.

	1998 Amounts as % of 1997 Amounts

2.

	1998		1997	
	Dollars	Percentage	Dollars	Percentage
Sales				
Sales returns				
Beginning inventories				
Cost of manufactured radios				
Ending inventories				
Cost of goods sold				
Selling expenses				
Administrative expenses				
Income before tax				

3.

E5–15

Current ratio =

Quick ratio =

Defensive interval =

E5–16

1.

2. Number of days' sales in
   average receivables =

Number of days' sales in
average inventory =

E5–17

Price-earnings ratio =

Dividend yield =

Dividend payout =

Common stockholders'
   return =

E5–18

Book value per share =

E5–19

1. Cash =

2. Average accounts receivable =

3. Average inventory =

4. Long-term debt =

Calculations:

P5–1

Schroeder Company

Balance Sheet

As of December 31, 1998

(in thousands)

Liabilities and Stockholders' Equity

Assets

P5–2

1.

DeBerg Industries, Inc.

Income Statement

For the Year Ended December 31, 1998

(in thousands)

**P5–2
(concluded)**

2.

DeBerg Industries, Inc.

Balance Sheet

As of December 31, 1998

(in thousands)

Assets

Liabilities and Stockholders' Equity

P5–3

Stolle Corporation

Balance Sheet

December 31, 1998

(in millions)

P5–4

Forest Products, Inc.

Balance Sheet

As of December 31, 1998

(in thousands)

Liabilities and Stockholders' Equity

Assets

P5–5

Houser Company

Balance Sheet

As of December 31, 1998

(in thousands)

Assets

P5-5 (concluded)

Liabilities and Stockholders' Equity

P5–8

1.

Jim and Joyce Company

Balance Sheet

As of December 31, 1998

Assets

Liabilities and Stockholders' Equity

P5–8 (concluded)

2.

Jim and Joyce Company

Income Statement

For the Year Ended December 31, 1998

P5–9

Calculations:

P5–9 (concluded)

Albrecht Company

Statement of Financial Position

November 30, 1998

P5–12

   1. Current (working capital) ratio =

   2. Profit margin on sales =

   3. Accounts receivable turnover =

      Number of days' sales =

   4. Inventory turnover =

   5. Book value per share =

   6. Earnings per share =

   7. Price-earnings ratio =

   8. Dividend payout ratio =

P5–13

1. Liquidity ratios:

Activity or turnover ratios:

Leverage ratios:

Profitability ratios:

2. a) Times interest earned =

b) Return on total assets =

c) Return on common stockholders' equity =

P5–13 (concluded)

d) Total liabilities to total assets =

e) Accounts receivable turnover =

f) Current ratio =

g) Quick ratio =

E6–1

1. a)

b)

2.

3.

4.

5.

6.

E6–2

Baker Corporation

Statement of Cash Flows

For the Year Ending December 31, 1998

E6–3

E6–4

E6–5

E6–6

E6–7

E6–8

E6–9

E6–10

E6–11

E6–12

E6–13

E6–14

Lindal Corporation

Balance Sheet

December 31, 1998

Assets

Liabilities and Stockholders' Equity

Calculations:

E6–15

E6–16

1.

2.

3.

E6–17

Patton Corporation

Income Statement

For the Year Ending November 30, 1998

Calculations:

E6–18

1. Sales revenue:

2. Depreciation expense:

3. Uncollectible accounts expense:

4. Wages expense:

5. Taxes expense:

6. Insurance expense:

7. Interest expense:

E6–18 (concluded)

   8. Net income:

E6–19

  (1)

  (2)

  (3)

  (4)

  (5)

  (6)

  (7)

  (8)

P6–1

   1. a) Cash collections from customers:

P6–1 (concluded)

1. b) Reconciliation of net income to cash provided by operating activities:

2.

Jackson Corporation

Statement of Cash Flows

For the Year Ending December 31, 1998

P6–2

Bolton, Inc.

Statement of Cash Flows

For the Year Ended December 31, 1998

Cash flows from operating activities:

Reconciliation of net income to net cash provided by operating activities:

P6–3

Victory Flower Shop

Statement of Cash Flows

For the Year Ended December 31, 1998

Cash flows from operating activities:

Investing and financing activities not affecting cash:

P6–4

1. Cash flows from operating activities:

2. Cash flows from investing activities:

3. Cash flows from financing activities:

P6–5

1. a)

P6–5 (concluded)

1. b) Reconciliation of net income to net cash provided by operating activities:

2.   Greer Company

Statement of Cash Flows

For the Year Ended December 31, 1998

Net cash provided by operating activities:									
(from part 1)					$		4	0	0
Cash flows from investing activities:									

Investing and financing activities not affecting cash:

P6–6

Knott Company

Statement of Cash Flows

For the Year Ended December 31, 1998

Cash flows from operating activities:

Reconciliation of net income to net cash provided by operating activities:

P6–7

Grand Hotel

Statement of Cash Flows

For the Year Ended December 31, 1998

Cash flows from operating activities:

Investing and financing activities not affecting cash:

Calculations:

P6–8

High Corporation

Statement of Cash Flows

For the Year Ended December 31, 1998

Cash flows from operating activities:

Reconciliation of net income to net cash provided by operating activities:

Calculations:

P6–9 Adjustments to Cash Basis

1.	Per Income Statement	Add	Deduct	Cash Basis

2. Cash flows from investing activities:

3. Cash flows from financing activities:

E7–1   Income for 1998 =

E7–2

   1.

   2.

E7–3

   1.

   2.

E7–4

	Percentage-of-Completion	Completed-Contract

E7–5

1.

	1998	1999

2. 1998:

	Debit	Credit

1999:

3. 1998:

1999:

E7–6	Debit	Credit
1.		

2.

3.

E7–6 (concluded)

	Debit	Credit
3. (continued)		

E7–7

1.

2.

	a)	b)	c)

E7–8

1.

Year	Cash Received From		Gross Profit Ratio	Income Recognized
	1998 Sales	1999 Sales		
1998				
1999				

2.

Year	Beginning Balance	+	Additions	–	Income Recognized	=	Ending Balance
1998							
1999							

3.

Year	Cash Received From		Unrecovered Cost		Income Recognized
	1998 Sales	1999 Sales	1998	1999	
1998					
1999					

E7–9

	1.	2.	3.
Revenue:			
Expenses:			
Net Income:			

E7–10

1.

Year	Gross Profit	Sales	Gross Profit Ratio
1998			
1999			
2000			

Year	Cash Collections	Gross Profit Ratio	Income Recognized
1998			
1999			
2000			

2.

Year	Cash Collections	Unrecovered Cost	Income Recognized
1998			
1999			
2000			

E7–11

1.

	Debit	Credit

E7–11 (concluded)

	Debit	Credit
1. continued		

1999

2.	1998	1999

3.	Debit	Credit

E7-12	Accts. Receivable	Deferred Gross Profit
1997 Sales		

E7-13

1. Recognition When Production is Complete:

   1998:

   1999:

   2000:

2. Recognition at Point of Sale:

   1998:

   1999:

   2000:

3. Recognition Under the Installment Method:

   1998:

   1999:

   2000:

E7–13 (concluded)

4. Recognition Under the Cost-Recovery Method:

Date	Cash Collected	–	Unrecovered Cost	=	Income
1998					
1999					
2000					

E7–14

1.

2. a)

	Debit	Credit

b)

c)

d)

e)

E7–15

		1998	1999	2000
1.	Contract price	$ 4 0 0 0 0 0 0	$ 4 0 0 0 0 0 0	$ 4 0 0 0 0 0 0

2.

	1998	1999	2000

E7–16

	Completed-Contract	Percentage-of-Completion
Balance sheet, end of year:		
Accounts receivable:		
1998		
1999		
Construction in progress, net of billings:		
1998		
1999		
Income statement, for the year:		
Construction revenue:		
1998		
1999		
Construction expenses:		
1998		
1999		

E7–17	Debit	Credit
1.		
2.		
3.		
4.		

E7–17 (concluded) | Debit | Credit

4. continued

5.

E7–18 | Debit | Credit

1.

2.

3.

4.

E7–19		Debit		Credit	
Jan. 15					
Jan. 31					
Mar. 10					
May 1					
Aug. 1					
Aug. 30					
Oct. 19					
Nov. 1					
Nov. 30					

Instructor ______ Section ______ Name ______

E7–20

	Debit	Credit
a)		
b)		
c)		
d)		

E7–21

	Debit	Credit
a)		
b)		
c)		

P7–1

1.	1998	1999	2000
a)			
b)			
c)			

2. Method a) At the completion of production:	Debit	Credit

P7–1 (concluded)	Debit	Credit
2. Method b) At the point of sale:		

3. Method c) As cash is collected:

P7–2	Completion of Production	Date of Sale
1. Revenue		

2. a) Completion of production:

b) Date of sale:

3.	Debit	Credit

P7–3	Debit	Credit
1. a)		
b)		
c)		
d)		
e)		
f)		

P7–3 (concluded)	**Debit**	**Credit**
g)		

2.   Record Exchange

Income Statement

For the Year Ended December 31, 1998

3.   Record Exchange

Balance Sheet

December 31, 1998

Assets

P7–4 | 1998 | 1999 | 2000

1.

2. Please see next page for part 2.

3. | 1998 | 1999 | 2000

Assets

P7–4 (concluded)

2.

	1998		1999		2000	
	Debit	Credit	Debit	Credit	Debit	Credit

P7–5	Debit	Credit
1.		

P7–5 (concluded)

2.

Buddys Bend State Park

Income Statement

For the Year Ending December 31, 1998

Buddys Bend State Park

Balance Sheet

As of December 31, 1998

Assets

P7–6

1. When production is complete:

   1998:

   1999:

   2000:

2. At point of sale:

Year	Selling Price/Unit	–	Cost/Unit	=	Gross Profit/Unit	Units Sold	Income Recognized
1998							
1999							
2000							

3. Installment method:

	Cash Collected	x	Percentage	=	Income Recognized
1998					
1999					
2000					

4. Cost-recovery method:

	Cash Collected	–	Unrecovered Cost	=	Income Recognized
1998					
1999					
2000					

P7–7

1.

Buddy's Fitness Center

Income Statements

For the Years Ended December 31

	1998	1999

P7–7 (concluded)

2.

Buddy's Fitness Center

Balance Sheet

December 31, 1998

3.

	Debit	Credit

P7–8

1. a) Completed-contract method:

Completed-Contract Project	Revenue	Expenses	Loss	Income (Loss) to be Reported
A				
C				
D				
Totals				

b) Percentage-of-completion method:

Percentage-of-Completion Project	Revenue (Schedule 1)	Expenses	Income (Loss) to Be Reported
A			
B			
C			
D			
E			
Totals			

Documentation: Schedule 1

Projects

A

B

C

D

E

2. 1) & 2)

3)

4)

5)

6)

P7–8 (concluded)

Documentation: Schedule 2 (Completed-Contract)

Project	Construction in Progress	Related Billings	Costs in Excess of Billings	Billings in Excess of Costs
A				
B				
D				
E				
Totals				

Schedule 3 (Percentage-of-Completion)

Project	Costs and Estimated Earnings (Losses)	Related Billings	Costs and Estimated Earnings in Excess of Billings	Billings in Excess of Costs and Estimated Earnings
A				
B				
D				
E				
Totals				

P7–9

1. a) Production basis:

	1998	1999	2000

b) Sales basis:

	1998	1999	2000

P7–9 (concluded)

  1. c) Installment basis:

2.   Alternative

Year	Production	Sales	Installment
1998			
1999			
2000			
Total			

P7–10

1.   Debit   Credit

Calculations:

Year	Accounts Receivable Beginning Balance	Accounts Receivable Ending Balance	Cash Collected	Gross Profit Ratio	Gross Profit Realized
1996					
1997					
1998					

P7–10 (concluded)

2.

	Debit	Credit

Calculations:

P7–11

1. 1998

	Debit	Credit

1999

P7–11 (concluded)

1. 1999 continued	Debit	Credit

2.   Stay and Pass (SAP)

Income Statements

For the Years Ended December 31

	1998	1999

3.   Stay and Pass (SAP)

Balance Sheets

December 31

Assets	1998	1999
Liabilities and capital		

P7–12

	May 31, 1998	May 31, 1999
1.		

2. Contracts	Number	Amount	Earned Portion	Recognize
one-year				
two-year				
three-year				

3.

P7–13

1.

Sho and Go

Income Statements

For the Years Ended December 31,

	1998	1999
Revenues		
Expenses:		
Net income		

P7–13 (concluded)

2.

Sho and Go

Balance Sheets

December 31

	1998	1999

Calculations:

P7–14 | | Debit | | Credit |

1.

P7–14 (concluded)

2.

Hardage Corporation

Income Statement

For the Year Ended December 31, 1998

3.

Hardage Corporation

Balance Sheet

December 31, 1998

Assets

Liabilities and Stockholders' Equity

P7–15

1.

2.   Debit   Credit

P7–15 (concluded)

3.

Cocoa Trading Corporation

Income Statement

For the Year Ended December 31, 1998

Cocoa Trading Corporation

Statement of Financial Position

December 31, 1998

P7–16 or P7–17	Debit	Credit
1.		

P7–16 or P7–17 (concluded)	**Debit**	**Credit**
1. cont.		

2.	Ross McAlister	
	Balance Sheet	
	Beginning of the Year	

E8—1

	Debit	Credit
1. May 1		
2. May 20		
3. May 27		

E8—2

1.

Pearson Company

Bank Reconciliation

Month of XXX

Balance per bank statement		
Balance per books		

2.	Debit	Credit

E8–3

Balance per bank statement, March 31

Balance per books, March 1

E8–4

1.

Arkansas Gazette

Bank Reconciliation

Month of September, 1998

Balance per bank statement, Sept. 30

2.

	Debit	Credit

E8–5

1.

	Debit	Credit
2. a)		
b)		
c)		

E8–6

1.

2.

E8–7

	Debit	Credit
1. a)		
b)		
c)		
d)		
Adjusting entry:		

E 8–7 (concluded)

2.

3.

	Debit	Credit

E8–8

1.

2.

E8–9

	Debit	Credit

E8–9 (concluded)

	Debit	Credit

E8–10

	Debit	Credit
1.		
2.		

E8–11

E8–12

	Debit	Credit
Mar. 3		
Mar. 12		
Mar. 17		
Mar. 26		
Apr. 15		

Instructor ______________ Section ______________ Name ______________

E8–13 — Debit / Credit

a)

b)

c)

d)

E8–14

	Debit	Credit
1.		

	Debit	Credit
2.		

E8–15

	Debit	Credit
Mar. 1		
Apr. 1		
May 1		

E8–16

	Debit	Credit
1.		

	Debit	Credit
2.		

E8–17   Debit   Credit

a)

b)

E8–18   Debit   Credit

1. Jul. 31

   Aug. 30

2.

E8–19   Debit   Credit

E8–20

a)

b)

c)

E8–21

	Debit	Credit
1. a)		
b)		
c)		
d)		
2.		

E8–22

1.

	Debit	Credit
2.		
3.		

E8–23

Liabilities:	

E8–26 | | **Debit** | **Credit**

1. a)

   b)

2. a)

   b)

E8–27 | | **Debit** | **Credit**

E8–28 | | **Debit** | **Credit**

Dec. 31, 1998 Accrual:

1999 Payment:

Dec. 31, 1999 Accrual:

E8–29 | | **Debit** | **Credit**

E8–30

1.

	Debit	Credit
2. Feb. 17		
Mar. 31		
Jun. 30		
Dec. 31		

E8–31

	Debit	Credit
1. Jan. 31		
Feb. 28		
Mar. 31		

2.

E8–32

1.

	Debit		Credit	
2.				

E8–33

1.	2.

E8–34

	Debit		Credit	
1.				
2.				

E8–37

E8–38

	Debit	Credit
1. 1998:		
a)		
b)		
c)		
1999:		
a)		
b)		
c)		

2. Estimated warranty liability:

1998 balance:

1999 balance:

E8–39

E8–40

	1998		1999	
	Debit	Credit	Debit	Credit
1.				
2.				
3.				

Calculations:

E8–41

1.		

2.	Debit	Credit

P8–1

1.

| Tillman Corporation |
| Bank Reconciliation |
| Month of December |

Balance per bank statement								

2.

	Debit					Credit			

P8–2

1.

Ireland Company

Bank Reconciliation

Month of June

Balance per bank statement

Ireland Company

Bank Reconciliation

Month of July

Balance per bank statement

2.   **Debit**   **Credit**

P8–3

1.

2.

Justin Corporation

Bank Reconciliation

Month of December, 1998

P8–4

	Debit			Credit		

1. Mar. 1

Mar. 19

Apr. 3

Apr. 20

2.

P8–5		Debit		Credit	
1.					
2.					

Calculations: _____

_____

_____

_____

P8–6

_____

_____

_____

_____

_____

_____

_____

_____

_____

_____

P8–7

1.

2.

3.

P8–8	Debit	Credit
Mar. 1		
July 1		
Dec. 1		

P8–9		Debit		Credit	
1. a)					
b)					
Calculations:					
c)					
2. a)					
b)					

P8–9 (concluded)

2. b) cont.	Debit	Credit
c)		

P8–10

	Debit	Credit
1. Apr. 1		
June 30		
Nov. 1		
Dec. 1		
Calculations:		

P8–10 (concluded)

2. Income Statement Effects:

3.

P8–11

	Debit	Credit
1.		
2.		
3.		

4. Income Statement:

	Month of July	Month of August

Balance Sheet:

	July 31	August 31

P8–12

Age Category	Amount in Category	Profitability of Noncollection	Estimated Uncollectible Amount
Net yet due			
Less than 30 days past due			
30–60 days past due			
61–120 days past due			
121–180 days past due			
Over 180 days past due			

2. Entry:

	Debit	Credit

P8–13

	Debit	Credit
1.		
2.		

P8–14	Debit	Credit
1. a)		
b)		
c)		
d)		
e)		
f)		
g)		
h)		
i)		
j)		

P8–14 (concluded)	Debit	Credit
1. continued		
k)		
l)		
2. Schedule of Transferred Receivables:		
3.		

P8–15	Debit	Credit
A. January 1, 1998, allowance for doubtful accounts	$ 4 0 0 0 0 0	
B.		
C.		

P8–16	Debit	Credit
a)		
b)		
c)		
d)		

P8–17	Debit	Credit
a)		
b)		

P8–17 (concluded)　　　　　　　　　　　　　　　　　　　　　Debit　　　　　Credit

c)

P8–18　　　　　　　　　　　　　　　　　　　　　　　1995　　　　　1994

1. Current receivables:

2. Ratio of current receivables to total assets:

3. Current receivables due from customers:

4. Customers receivables turnover:

5.

6.

7.

Instructor ______________________ Section ______________ Name ______________________

P8–19 or P8–20

	Debit	Credit

P8–21	Debit	Credit
1. a)		
b)		
c)		
d)		
e)		
2.		

P8–23

1.		J. Alden		P. Watson		M. Fields		S. Golden
Wages for June	$	8 0 0 0	$	5 5 0 0	$	4 0 0 0	$	3 0 0 0
Federal income tax withheld								
Employer FICA taxes								
Employee FICA taxes								
State Unemployment								
Federal Unemployment								

2.	Debit	Credit
3.		

P8–24

1.

2.

3.	Debit	Credit

P8–25

1.

2.

	Debit	Credit
3. Feb. 20		
Apr. 30		
Jul. 1		
Dec. 31		

P8–26

	Debit	Credit
1. a)		
b)		
2. Quarterly at 3/31, 6/30, 9/30, 12/31:		

P8–26 (concluded)

3. a) President's bonus:

	Debit	Credit
b)		

4. Calculation of taxes:

	Debit	Credit

P8–28

	Debit	Credit
1. a)		
b)		
c)		
d)		

2. Income Statement:

Balance Sheet:

P8–30 or P8–31

	Debit	Credit

Instructor ______ Section ______ Name ______

P8–32 or P8–33

	Debit	Credit

E9–2

Unadjusted inventory balance on 12/31/98															$	7	1	3 0 0	

E9–4

Calculation of cost of goods sold:

Entries:	Debit	Credit

E9–5

1. Cost per unit of Model A:

Cost per unit of Model B:

E9–5 (concluded)

Cost per unit of Model C:

_____

_____

_____

_____

	Debit	Credit
2. a)		
b)		
3. a)		
b)		

E9–6

	Inventory	Accounts Payable	Sales
Unadjusted balances:	$ 3 8 3 5 0 0	$ 2 9 0 0 0	$ 8 6 5 0 0 0
Adjustments:			
a)			
b)			
c)			
d)			
e)			
Adjusted balances:			

E9–7

	Debit	Credit
a)		
b)		
c)		

E9–10

e) Purchases | $ | 1 4 1 0 0 0

Adjustments:

f) Income before tax | $ | 2 5 0 0 0

Adjustments:

g) Accounts payable | $ | 3 0 0 0 0

Adjustments:

h) Inventory | $ | 4 0 0 0 0

Adjustments:

E9–11

Calculations:

1. Reported income | $ | 2 0 0 0 0

Correct 1998 net income

2. | | Debit | Credit

E9–12

1. Moving average method:

	Units	Unit Cost	Total Cost	Moving Average Cost

2. Weighted average method:

E9–13

1. FIFO:

2. LIFO:

E9–13 (concluded)

3. Weighted average:

E9–14 or E9–15

	Debit	Credit

E9–16

1. Perpetual system:

   a) FIFO: Cost of goods sold:

   b) LIFO:

Date	Transaction	Cost of Goods Purchased	Cost of Goods Sold	Cumulative Balance of Inventory
1/1	Beg. inv.			250 @ $10.50 $ 2 6 2 5

2. Periodic system:

   a) FIFO:

   b) LIFO:

E9–17

1. a) FIFO:

    b) LIFO:

    c) Weighted average cost:

2.   Partial Income Statement

	FIFO		LIFO		Weighted Average	
Sales	$ 2 6 0 0 0 0 0		$ 2 6 0 0 0 0 0		$ 2 6 0 0 0 0 0	

E9–18

Calculation of ending inventory in units:

    a) FIFO:

E9–18 (concluded)

   b) LIFO:

   c) Average cost:

E9–19

   1. Ending inventory in units:

     a) FIFO:

     b) LIFO:

     c) Average cost:

   2.

E9-20

Dollar-Value LIFO

Date	Inventory At Current Year Costs	Inventory At Base Year Costs	Inventory Layers At Base Year Costs	Inventory Layers Restated	Dollar-Value LIFO Inventory
Jan. 1. 1998 (base)					
Dec. 31, 1998					
Dec. 31, 1999					
Dec. 31, 2000					

E9-21

Dollar-Value LIFO

Date	Inventory At Current Year Costs	Inventory At Base Year Costs	Inventory Layers At Base Year Costs	Inventory Layers Restated	Dollar-Value LIFO Inventory
1. Dec. 31, 1998					
2. Dec. 31, 1999					

3.

E9-22

Date	Inventory At Current Year Costs	Inventory At Base Year Costs	Inventory Layers At Base Year Costs	Inventory Layers Restated	Dollar-Value LIFO Inventory
Dec. 31. 1997 (base)					
Dec. 31, 1998					
Dec. 31, 1999					
Dec. 31, 2000					

E9-23

1.

	Debit	Credit

2. Balance sheet presentation:

P9–1 or P9–2

1.

	Debit	Credit

P9–1 or P9–2 (concluded)	Debit	Credit

P9–5

Master Corporation

Schedule of Adjustments

December 31, 1998

	Inventory	Accounts Payable	Sales
Inital Amounts	$1,2000,000	$985,000	$9,3000,000
Adjustments—increase (decrease)			
a)			
b)			
c)			
d)			
e)			
f)			
g)			
Total adjustments			
Adjusted amounts	$	$	$

P9–6

Jasper Corporation

Schedule of Adjustments

December 31, 1998

	Inventory	Accounts Payable	Sales
Inital Amounts	$1,8000,000	$1,100,000	$8,3000,000
Adjustments—increase (decrease)			
a)			
b)			
c)			
d)			
e)			
f)			
g)			
h)			
Total adjustments			
Adjusted amounts	$	$	$

P9–7

1. a)

P9–7(concluded)

b)

c)

d)

e)

f)

g)

2. Beginning inventory for 1998									$		1	8	7	0	0		

P9–8   **Debit**   **Credit**

1. June 4

   June 10

   June 15

   June 20

   June 23

2.

3.

4.

P9–9

	Assets	Liabilities	Retained Earnings
1. a)			
b)			
c)			
d)			
2. Reported net income			$ 3 8 0 0 0

P9–11

1. Periodic:

   a) FIFO:

   b) LIFO:

   c) Average cost:

2. Perpetual inventory system:

   a) FIFO:

   b) LIFO:

Date	Transaction	Cost of Goods Purchased			Cost of Goods Sold			Cumulative Balance of Inventory		
1/1	Beg. inv.							110 @ $5.25		5 7 7 5 0

P9–11 (concluded)

2. b) (continued)

Date	Transaction	Cost of Goods Purchased		Cost of Goods Sold		Cumulative Balance of Inventory	

c) Moving average:

	Units	Unit Cost	Total Cost	Moving Average Cost
Jan.1 – Beginning inventory	110	$	5 7 7 5 0 $	5 2 5

Instructor ____________ Section ____________ Name ____________

P9–12

1. a) FIFO:

b) LIFO:

c) Weighted average:

2.

	Debit	Credit
a)		

P9–12 (concluded) | Credit | Debit

2. a) (continued)

b) LIFO: (Note: Prepare only those entries that change and are different from part a.)

P9–13

1. a) FIFO:

   June:

   July:

   August:

   b) LIFO:

   June:

   July:

   August:

P9–13 (concluded)

   c) Weighted average:

      June:

      July:

      August:

2. Summary of gross profits:

	June	July	August
FIFO			
LIFO			
Weighted average			

Comments:

P9–14

FIFO:

LIFO:

Weighted average:

P9–15

1. Periodic inventory system:

   a) FIFO:

P9–15 (continued)

1. a) FIFO: (continued)

   b) Average cost:

   c) LIFO:

2. Perpetual inventory system:

   a) FIFO:

P9–15 (continued)

  2. Perpetual inventory system (cont.)

      b) Moving weighted average:

	Units	Unit Cost	Total Cost	Moving Average

      c) Please see next page for part 2c.

  3.

P9–15 (concluded)

2. c) LIFO:

Date	Transaction	Cost of Goods Puchased			Cost of Goods Sold			Cumulative Balance Of Inventory		
9/1	Beginning inventory:							200 @ $3.00	$	6 0 0 00

P9–16

1. Book inventory at November 30, 1998											$		6	0	0	0	0	

2. Correct physical inventory at November 30, 1998											$		5	8	0	0	0	

P9–18

1.

2. a) LIFO pool:

   b) Dollar value LIFO method:

   c) LIFO increment:

   d) LIFO valuation allowance:

P9–18 (concluded)	Current Year Ending Inventory	Ending Inventory at Base Year Prices
3. a) Dollar-value LIFO:		
b) Effect of change on pretax income:		
Effect of change on income taxes:		

P9–19 or P9–20

Dollar-Value

Date	Inventory At Current Year Costs	Inventory At Base Year Costs	Inventory Layers At Base Year Costs	Inventory Layers Restated	LIFO Inventory
Dec. 31, 1997 (base)					
Dec. 31, 1998					
Dec. 31, 1999					
Dec. 31, 2000					

P9–21

Date	Inventory At Current Year Costs	Inventory At Base Year Costs	Inventory Layers At Base Year Costs	Inventory Layers Restated	Dollar-Value LIFO Inventory
July 31. 1997 (base)					
July 31, 1998					
July 31, 1999					
July 31, 2000					
July 31, 2001					

E10–1

Product	Replacement Cost	Ceiling (NRV)	Floor (NRV – Normal Profit)	Market	Cost	LCM
1	$	$	$	$	$	$
2						

E10–2

Item	Replacement Cost	Ceiling	Floor	Market	Cost	LCM
1	$	$	$	$	$	$
2						
3						
4						

E10–3

1. Item	Replacement Cost	Ceiling	Floor	Market	Cost
A	$	$	$	$	$
B					
C					
D					
E					

2. and 3.			Lower of Cost or Market Applied to:		
Item	Cost	Market	Individual Items	Group of Items	Total Inventory
A					
B					
C					
D					
E					
Total					

E10–4

1. Item	Replacement Cost	Ceiling	Floor	Market	Cost
1					
2					
3					
4					
5					
6					

E10–4 (concluded)

2. and 3. Item	Cost	Market	Lower of Cost or Market Applied to:		
			Individual Items	Group of Items	Total Inventory
2					
5					
6					
1					
3					
4					
Total					

E10–5 or E10–6

	Debit	Credit

E10–7

E10–8

E10–9

E10–10

1.

2.

E10–11 or E10–12 | Cost | Retail

E10–13 or E10–14 | Cost | Retail

E10–15 or E10–16 | Cost | Retail

Instructor ________________ Section ________________ Name ________________

E10–17

	Cost	Retail

2.

3.

4.

	Cost	Retail

E10–18 or E10–19

	Cost										Retail									

(1) Ending Inventory Stated in Terms of Base Retail Prices	(2) Inventory Layers Stated in Terms of Base Retail Prices	(3) Inventory Layers Restated Using Proper Retail Price Indexes	(4) Inventory Layers Stated in Terms of Cost	(5) Dollar-Value Retail LIFO Ending Inventory

E10–20 or E10–21

1998:

	Cost		Retail

(1) Ending Inventory Stated in Terms of Base Retail Prices	(2) Inventory Layers Stated in Terms of Base Retail Prices	(3) Inventory Layers Restated Using Proper Retail Price Indexes	(4) Inventory Layers Stated in Terms of Cost	(5) Dollar-Value Retail LIFO Ending Inventory

1999:

	Cost		Retail

(1) Ending Inventory Stated in Terms of Base Retail Prices	(2) Inventory Layers Stated in Terms of Base Retail Prices	(3) Inventory Layers Restated Using Proper Retail Price Indexes	(4) Inventory Layers Stated in Terms of Cost	(5) Dollar-Value Retail LIFO Ending Inventory

P10–1

1.	Item	Replacement Cost	Ceiling	Floor	Market	Cost	LCM
	A						
	B						
	C						
	D						
	E						
	F						

2.

		Debit	Credit
a)	Alternative A:		
b)	Alternative B:		
c)	Alternative C:		

3.	Items	Cost	Market	LCM
	A			
	B			
	C			
	D			
	E			
	F			
	Total			

4.

P10–4

P10–5

P10–6 or P10–7

1.

2.

3.

Instructor ______________________ Section ______________ Name ______________________

P10–8 or P10–9

	Cost	Retail
1.		

2.

P10–10 or P10–11 | | Cost | | Retail |

1.

2.

3.

P10–12	Cost	Retail
1. Average cost:		
2. Lower of cost or market:		
3. LIFO:		

P10–13 or P10–14

1.

	Cost	Retail

2.

(1) Ending Inventory Stated in Terms of Base Retail Prices	(2) Inventory Layers Stated in Terms of Base Retail Prices	(3) Inventory Layers Restated Using Proper Retail Price Indexes	(4) Inventory Layers Stated in Terms of Cost	(5) Dollar-Value Retail LIFO Ending Inventory

P10–15

1.

	Cost		Retail

2.

	(1) Ending Inventory At Base Retail Prices	(2) Inventory Layers Stated in Terms of Base Retail Prices	(3) Inventory Layers Restated Using Proper Retail Price Indexes	(4) Inventory Layers Stated in Terms of Cost	(5) Dollar-Value Retail LIFO Ending Inventory
1998					
1999					

P10–16 or P10–17			Cost						Retail				
1.													
2.													

P10–16 or P10–17 (concluded)

3. 1998:

		Cost		Retail

(1) Ending Inventory Stated in Terms of Base Retail Prices	(2) Inventory Layers Stated in Terms of Base Retail Prices	(3) Inventory Layers Restated Using Proper Retail Price Indexes	(4) Inventory Layers Stated in Terms of Cost	(5) Dollar-Value Retail LIFO Ending Inventory

1999:

		Cost		Retail

(1) Ending Inventory Stated in Terms of Base Retail Prices	(2) Inventory Layers Stated in Terms of Base Retail Prices	(3) Inventory Layers Restated Using Proper Retail Price Indexes	(4) Inventory Layers Stated in Terms of Cost	(5) Dollar-Value Retail LIFO Ending Inventory

P10–18

	Year 1			Year 2		
	Cost		Retail	Cost		Retail

(1) End of Year	(2) Ending Inventory Stated in Terms of Base Retail Prices	(3) Inventory Layers Stated in Terms of Base Retail Prices	(4) Inventory Layers Restated Using Proper Retail Price Indexes	(5) Inventory Layers Stated in Terms of Cost	(6) Dollar-Value Retail LIFO Ending Inventory
1					
2					

E11–3

E11–4

1.

2.   Debit   Credit

E11–5

1.

2.

3.   Debit   Credit

E11–6

1.

2.

3.   Debit   Credit

E11–7 or E11–8

1.

2.

	Debit	Credit

3.

E11–9

E11–10

Sterling Corporation

Balance Sheet–Intangibles Section

As of December 31, 1998

E11–11

	Debit	Credit

1.

2.

E11–12 or E11–13

E11–14

E11–15 or E11–16

	Debit	Credit

E11–17 or E11–18

E11–19	Debit	Credit

E11–20 or E11–21	Debit	Credit

E11–22 or E11–23	Debit	Credit

E11–24 or E11–25	Debit	Credit

P11–1 or P11–2   **Debit**   **Credit**

P11–3   **Debit**   **Credit**

P11–4

1. 1997:

1998:

2. 1997:

1998:

	Debit	Credit

3.

P11–5

P11–6

1. 1998:

1999:

P11–6 (concluded)

2. Weighted average interest rate:

1998:

1999:

	Debit	Credit
3. 1998:		
1999:		

4.

P11–7 or P11–8	Debit	Credit

P11–7 or P11–8 (concluded)	Debit	Credit

P11–9 or P11–10		
1.		

P11–9 or P11–10 (concluded)

P11–11

	Debit	Credit
1. Hoyt:		
2. Cottell:		

P11–12

	Debit	Credit
1. a) Hoyt:		

P11–12 (concluded)	**Debit**	**Credit**
b) Cottel:		

2.

P11–13	**Debit**	**Credit**
Rahman:		
Ruland:		

P11–14 1. Land | 2. Buildings

1. Land				2. Buildings			
Beg. balance		$1 2 0 0 0 0 0		Beg. balance		$ 9 0 0 0 0 0	

P11–14 (concluded)

3. Leasehold Improvements	4. Machinery and Equipment

P11–15	Debit	Credit
a)		
b)		
c)		
d)		
e)		
f)		
g)		

Calculations:

E12–1 or E12–2

_____

_____

_____

_____

_____

_____

_____

_____

_____

_____

_____

_____

_____

_____

_____

_____

_____

_____

_____

_____

_____

_____

E12–3	**1998**	**1999**
1. Straight-line method:		
2. Sum-of-the-years'-digits method:		
3. Double-declining-balance method:		

E12–4	**1998**
1. Straight-line method:	
2. Sum-of-the-years'-digits method:	
3. Double-declining-balance method:	
4. Production method:	
5. Use method:	

E12–6 | | Debit | Credit

1.

2.

3.

Calculations:	Year	Payment	Interest	Prin. Reduction	Balance
	1998				
	1999				
	2000				

E12–7 or E12–8

1.

Asset	Acquisition Cost	Salvage Value	Depreciation Base	Useful Life	Straight-Line Depr./Year

2. | Debit | Credit

E12–9 | Debit | Credit

1.

2.

E12–10 or E12–11

E12–12

E12–13 or E12–14

E12–15

E12–16

1.

2.

E12–17 or E12–18 | Debit | Credit

E12–20

1.

2.

3.

P12–1 or P12–2	Debit	Credit

P12–3

	1998	**1999**
1. Straight-line method:		
2. Sum-of-the-years'-digits method:		
3. Double-declining-balance method:		
4. Use method:		

P12–4

			Depr. Expense	Accum. Depr.
1.	Year:	1996		
		1997		
		1998		

			Depr. Expense	Accum. Depr.
2.				
	Year:	1996		
		1997		
		1998		

P12–5

1.

Analysis of Land Account – 1998

Balance at January 1, 1998	$	3 0 0 0 0 0

2.

Analysis of Land Improvements Account – 1998

Balance at January 1, 1998	$	9 0 0 0 0

3.

Analysis of Buildings Account – 1998

Balance at January 1, 1998	$	9 0 0 0 0 0

P12–5 (concluded)

4.   Analysis of Machinery and Equipment Account – 1998

Balance at January 1, 1998		$ 5 5 0 0 0 0

P12–7 or P12–8   Debit   Credit

1.

2.

3.

4.

5.

P12–9	Debit	Credit
Machine *X*:		
Machine *Y*:		
Machine *Z*:		

P12–10

1998:

1999:

P12–11

1. Calculation of depletion base:		

1998:

1999:

2.	Debit	Credit
1998:		

P12–11 (concluded)

2. 1999:

	Debit	Credit

P12–12

	Debit	Credit
a)		
b)		
c)		
d)		
e)		

P12–13

1. Intangibles Section of Balance Sheet As of December 31, 1998

P12–13 (concluded)

2.   Income Statement Effect For the Year Ended December 31, 1998

Supporting calculations for parts 1 and 2:

P12–14	Debit	Credit

P12–15

Calculation of Goodwill and Accumulated Amortization At December 31, 1999

	Goodwill	Accumulated Amortization
Moore Company:		
Powell Company:		

Supporting calculations:

Schedule I-Calculation of Goodwill-Powell Company

Calculation of Goodwill Amortization For the Year Ended December 31, 1999

P12–16   Capitalized cost of building: Capitalized cost of land:

a)

Number of years: Number of years:

b) Capitalized cost of conveyor: Capitalized cost of TMS:

Number of years: Number of years:

c) Capitalized cost of trademark: Number of years:

d) Capitalized cost of patent: Number of years:

e) Capitalized cost: Number of years:

P12–18	Debit	Credit
a)		
b)		
c)		
d)		
e)		

E13–1   Debit   Credit

a)

b)

E13–2   Debit   Credit

1.

2.

E13–3   Debit   Credit

1.

2.

E13–4

1. a)

	Debit	Credit

   b)

	Debit	Credit

2.

3.

E13–5

	Debit	Credit

E13–6

1.

	Debit	Credit

2.

3. End of 1998:

E13–6 (concluded)

3. End of 1999:

4.

5.

	Debit	Credit

E13–7

	Debit	Credit
1.		

2. End of 1998:

End of 1999:

E13–8 Debit Credit

E13–9 or E13–10 Debit Credit

1.

2.

E13–9 or E13–10 (concluded)	Debit	Credit
2. continued		

E13–11 or E13–12	Debit	Credit
1.		
2.		

E13–13	Debit	Credit

E13–13 (concluded) | Debit | Credit

E13–14 or E13–15 | Debit | Credit

1.

2.

Instructor ______ Section ______ Name ______

E13–16 or E13–17

	Debit	Credit

E13–18 or E13–19

	Debit	Credit

P13–1	Debit	Credit
a)		
b)		
c)		
d)		

P13–2 or E13–3	Debit	Credit
1.		

P13–2 or P13–3 (concluded) Debit Credit

2.

3.

P13–4 or P13–5 Debit Credit

1.

2.

P13–4 or P13–5 (concluded)	Debit	Credit
2.		
3.		

P13–6 or P13–7	Debit	Credit
1.		

P13–6 or P13–7 (continued)	Debit	Credit

P13–6 or P13–7 (concluded)	Debit	Credit

P13–8

1.   **Investment in McKnight–Common - November 30, 1998**

2.   **Equity in Subsidiary Earnings - Year Ended November 30, 1998**

P13–9 or P13–10   Debit   Credit

1.

P13–9 or P13–10 (concluded)	Debit	Credit

P13–10

3. **Schedule of Investment in Sepe Corporation Common - December 31, 1998**

P13–11 **Goodwill and Accumulated Amortization - Year Ending December 31, 1998**

	Goodwill	Accumulated Amortization
White Company:		
Jabara Company:		

P13–12

Bradley Company Common Stock		Debit		Credit	

Mori, Inc. Common and Preferred Stock					

P13–12 (concluded)	**Debit**	**Credit**
Grace Service, Inc. Common Stock		
Pinto Instruments, Inc. Common Stock		

Supporting schedules:

P13–13

1.

Schedule of Trading Securities - December 31, 1998

2.

Schedule of Long-Term Investments - December 31, 1998

Supporting calculations:

P13–14

1.

2.

Schedule of Income from Investment in Park Using the Equity Method For Years Ended December 31, 1999 & 1998

	1999	1998

P13–15	Debit	Credit
1.		
2.		

Calculations:

E14–1

Issue	Principal	Interest	Total Selling Price
1.			
2.			
3.			
4.			

Journal entries:	Debit	Credit
Issue 1:		
Issue 2:		
Issue 3:		
Issue 4:		

E14–2

1.

2. _____ nominal interest _____ effective interest _____

3.

	Debit	Credit
a)		
b)		

E14–3

1.

2.

Year Ending	Interest Expense	Increase in Book Value	Book Value of Notes
3-1-99			
3-1-00			
3-1-01			
3-1-02			
3-1-03			

E14–3 (concluded)

3.

	Debit	Credit

E14–4

1. a) Market rate of 6%:

  b) Market rate of 10%:

2.

	Debit	Credit
a)		
b)		
3.		

E14–5

1.

Year Ending	Interest Expense	Cash	Decrease in Book Value	Book Value
12-31-98				
12-31-99				
12-31-00				
12-31-01				
12-31-02				

2.

	Debit	Credit

E14–6

1.

2. Tyson (issuer):

	Debit	Credit

Weaver (investor):

E14–7

1. For 1998:

For 1999:

2.

E14–8

	Debit	Credit
1.		
2.		
3.		
4.		
5.		

Six Months Ending	Interest Revenue	Cash	Increase in Book Value	Book Value
4-30-99				
10-31-99				

E14–9

Date	Interest Revenue	Cash	Increase in Book Value	Book Value
4-30-99				
10-31-99				
Sale				
4-30-00				

1. For 1998:

For 1999:

2.

E14–10

	Debit	Credit
1.		
2.		
3.		
4.		

Year Ending	Interest Expense	Cash	Increase in Book Value	Book Value
5/31/99				
5/31/00				
5/31/01				
5/31/02				
5/31/03				
5/31/04				

Instructor ______________________ Section ______________ Name ______________________

E14–11

1.

2.

	Debit	Credit

E14–12 or E14–13

	Debit	Credit

E14–14

Present Value of

	Principal	+	Interest	=	Total
(Matures 12/31/99)					
(Matures 12/31/00)					
(Matures 12/31/01)					

2.

Year	Interest Expense	Cash	Increase in Book Value	Par Value Maturing	Book Value
1998					
1999					
2000					
2001					

E14–15 or E14–16

1.	Debit	Credit

2.		

3.	Debit	Credit

E14–17 or E14–18

1. _____

	Debit	Credit
2.		
3.		

E14–19 or E14–20

	Debit	Credit

E14–21

	1998		1999	
	Debit	Credit	Debit	Credit
1.				
2.				

E14–22 or E14–23

1.

	Debit	Credit

E14–24

	Debit	Credit

	Debit	Credit

E14–25 or E14–26	Debit	Credit
1.		
2.		
3.		

E14–27	Debit	Credit

E14–28 or E14–29 | Debit | Credit

E14–30 or E14–31 or E14–32 | Debit | Credit

P14–1

1.

Year Ending Dec. 31	Interest Expense	Cash	Decrease in Book Value	Book Value
1998				
1999				
2000				
2001				
2002				
2003				
2004				
2005				
2006				
2007				

2.

	Debit	Credit

3.

4.

P14–2

1.

	Debit	Credit

2.

Year Ending Dec. 31	Interest Revenue	Cash	Increase in Book Value	Book Value
2001				
2002				
2003				
2004				
2005				
2006				
2007				

P14–2 (concluded)

	Debit	Credit
3.		
4.		
5.		

P14–3

	Debit	Credit
1. a)		
b)		
c)		
2.		

P14–4 or P14–5

	Debit	Credit

P14–4 or P14–5 (concluded)	Debit	Credit

P14–6

1.	End of Year	Interest Expense/Revenue	Cash	Decrease in Book Value	Book Value
	1998				
	1999				
	2000				

2. Chance Motors (issuer):

	Debit	Credit

P14–6 (concluded)

	Debit	Credit

2. Issuer (continued):

Wayne Investment Company (Investor):

3.

P14–7

End of Year	Interest Revenue	Cash	Increase in Book Value (Amortization)	Book Value
1998				
1999				
2000				
2001				

Other calculations:

P14–7 (continued)   Debit   Credit

Entries:

P14–7 (concluded)

	Debit	Credit

P14–8 or P14–10

Period	Interest	Cash	Change in Book Value	Book Value

	Debit	Credit

P14–9

1.

2. a)

End of Year		Cash Flow		Factor		Present Value	
1							
2							
3							
4							
5							
6							
7							
8							
9							
10							

b) Interest revenue recorded at:

	Year 1	Year 2
Year 1:		
Year 2:		
Correct interest revenue		
Year 1:		
Year 2:		
Over/under statement		

c) Notes receivable as reported:

Year 1:		
Year 2:		
Notes receivable correct amount:		
Year 1:		
Year 2:		
Over/under statement		

P14–10 - combined with P14–8 on previous page

P14–11 or P14–12

	Debit	Credit

P14–13

1. End of Year	Cash Flow	Pn7 12%	Present Value
3			
4			
5			
6			
7			
8			
Total			

Calculation of cash flows:

Year	3	4	5	6	7	8
Principal						
Interest						

P14–13 (concluded)

2.

End of Year	Interest Expense	Cash Interest	Increase in Book Value	Principal Maturing	Book Value
2					
3					
4					
5					
6					
7					
8					

3.

	Debit	Credit

P14–14

1.

	Debit	Credit

2.

3.

	Debit	Credit

P14–14 (concluded)	Debit	Credit
3. (continued)		

P14–15	1/1/98	12/31/98	12/31/99	12/31/00
1. Fair values:				
Derivative				
Bond investment				
2. Changes in FV:				
Derivative				
Bond investment				
3. Income statements				
4.				

P14–16

	Debit	Credit

a)

b)

	Debit	Credit

E15–1

	Case 1	Case 2	Case 3	Case 4

E15–2 or E15–3

1.

Year	Interest Revenue/Expense	Annual Lease Payment	Reduction in Receivable/Payable	Receivable/Payable Balance (End of Year)
1998				
1999				
2000				
2001				

2. Alaina Corporation (Lessor)   Nebo Consulting (Lessee)

January 1, 1998

	Debit	Credit		Debit	Credit

December 31, 1998

	Debit	Credit		Debit	Credit

E15–2 or E15–3 (concluded)   December 31, 1998

2. Cont.	Debit	Credit	Debit	Credit

December 31, 1999

	Debit	Credit	Debit	Credit

3.	Alaina Corporation		Nebo Consulting	

E15–4

Year	Interest Revenue/Expense	Annual Lease Payment	Reduction in Receivable/Liability	Balance of Receivable/Liability Liability (End of Year)
1				
2				
3				
4				

E15–7 (concluded)   Debit   Credit

4. continued

E15–8   Debit   Credit

1. Lessor:

Lessee:

E15–8 (concluded)

2.	Year	Annual Lease Payments	Outstanding during Year	Interest Expense	Reduction in Receivable	Balance (End of Year)
Lessor:						
	1					
	2					
	3					
	4					

	Year	Annual Lease Payments	Liability Outstanding during Year	Interest Expense	Reduction in Liability	Liability Balance (End of Year)
Lessee:						
	1					
	2					
	3					
	4					

3.		Debit	Credit

E15–9 or E15–10 or E15–11

	Debit	Credit

E15–9 or E15–10 or E15–11 (concluded) | Debit | Credit

E15–12 | 1. 10% | 2. 12%

E15–13 or E15–14 | Debit | Credit

E15–13 or E15–14 (concluded)

	Debit	Credit

E15–15 or E15–16 | | Debit | Credit

1.

2.

E15–17 | | Debit | Credit

E15–18 is on the next page

E15–19

E15–18 or E15–20

1.

2.

15–1 or P15–2

1.

2.		Debit		Credit	

3.

4.

P15–3 or P15–4

1.

2.

P15–3 or P15–4 (concluded)

3.

4.

P15–5 or P15–6

1.

2.

3. | | Debit | Credit |
|---|---|---|

4.

Year	Annual Lease Payments	Receivable/Payable Outstanding during Year	Interest Revenue/Expense	Reduction in Receivable/ Payable	Receivable/ Payable Balance (End of Year)
1998					
1999					
2000					
2001					
2002					

P15–5 or P15–6 (concluded) | Debit | Credit

P15–7 or P15–8

1.

2. | Debit | Credit

P15–7 or P15–8 (concluded)	Debit	Credit
2. (continued)		

3.	Debit	Credit

4. (P15–8 only)

Assets:		Liabilities:	

5. (P15–8 only)	Debit	Credit

P15–9

1.

2.

	Debit	Credit

3.

P15–10 or P15–12

1.

2.

	Debit	Credit

P15–10 or P15–12 (continued)

	Debit	Credit

3.

P15–10 or P15–12 (concluded)

	Debit	Credit
4.		

P15–11

		Credit
1.		

2.

3. a) SSI (lessor):	Debit	Credit
KIC (lessee):		

P15–11 (concluded)		Debit		Credit
3. a) (continued)				
b) SSI (lessor):				
KIC (lessee):				

P15–13 or P15–14

1.

2. (P15–13 only) Period	Interest	Lease Payments	Reduction in Liability	Balance of Liability
1				
2				
3				
4				

		Debit		Credit
3.				

P15–13 or P15–14 (concluded)   Debit   Credit

3. (continued)

4. (P15–13 only)

P15–15

1.

2.   Debit   Credit

3.

4.

P15–16 or P15–17		Debit	Credit
1.			

P15–16 or P15–17 (concluded)	Debit	Credit

E16–1 or E16–2

1.

2.

E16–3

E16–4 or E16–5

1.

2.

E16–6	Debit	Credit
1. Year 1:		

E16–6 (concluded)

	Debit	Credit
1. Year 2:		

2.

3.

	End of Yr. 1	Debit	Credit	End of Yr. 2

E16–7

	Service Cost		ABO
1. 1998:			
1999:			

2.

E16–8

1998:

1999:

2000:

E16–9

1.

2.   Debit   Credit

3.

E16–10   End of 1997   Debit   Credit   End of 1998

E16–11	Year	Projected	Actual	Gain (Loss)
1.	1995			
	1996			
	1997			
	1998			
	1999			
	2000			

2.		Cum. Unrecog. Gain (Loss)	Amount of Amortization

3.

E16–12

1.

	Cum. Unrecog. Gain (Loss)	Amount of Amortization

2. 1998:

    1999:

E16–13 or E16–14

	Debit	Credit

E16–15

1.

2.

3.

E16–16

	1998	1999	2000

E16–17

E16–18 or E16–19

E16–18 or E16–19 (concluded)

E16–20

	1/1/98	Debit	Credit	12/31/98

E16–22

	Case 1	Case 2	Case 3	Case 4

P16–1

1.

2.

3.

4.

	Year 1	Year 2

5.

	Year 1	Year 2

P16–2 or P16–3

1.

P16–4

1.

2.

3.

4.

5.

	Debit	Credit

P16–5

1.

	Calculations	Total Expected Annual Benefit
Davis:		
Estes:		
Manor:		
Total		

2. Calculation of pension expense:

	1998	1999

Service cost calculations:

P16–5 (concluded)   Debit   Credit

3. 1998:

   1999:

4.

P16–6

1.

2.

3.

Year	Service Cost	Interest Cost	Return on Plan Assets	Prior Service Cost Amort.	Net Pension Expense	Funding	Projected Benefit Obligation	Plan Assets
1998								
1999								
2000								

4.   Debit   Credit

   1998:

   1999:

P16–6 (concluded)   Debit   Credit

4. 2000:

5.

P16–7 or P16–8

1.

2.

3.

P16–9

	Year 1		Year 2	
1.	Debit	Credit	Debit	Credit

Calculation of pension expense:

	Year 1	Year 2

2. Balance sheet:

Income statement:

3.

P16–10 or P16–11

	1998	1999
1.		

Calculations:

Projected benefit obligation:

	1998	1999

Plan assets:

P16–10 or P16–11 (concluded)	Debit	Credit
2. 1/1/98:		
12/31/98:		
12/31/99:		
3.		
4.		
5.		

P16–12 and P16–13 are on the next page.

P16–14	Debit	Credit

Instructor ______________________ Section ______________ Name ______________________

P16–12 or P16–13

	Beginning	Debit	Credit	Ending
1.				

2.

P16–15

1.

Date	EPBO	Service Cost	APBO
1/1/98			
12/31/98			
12/31/99			
12/31/00			
12/31/01			
12/31/02			

2.

Postretirement

Year	Service Cost	Interest Cost	Benefit Expense	APBO
1998				
1999				
2000				
2001				
2002				

P16–16

1.

2. Projected Benefit Obligation:

	1996	1997	1998	1999

Plan Assets:

P16–16 (continued)

3. 1996:

	Debit	Credit

1997:

1998:

1999:

4.

Years Ending	Dec. 31, 1997	Dec. 31, 1998

P16–16 (concluded)

5.

6.

P16–17

1. Income statement:

Balance sheet:

2.

	Debit	Credit

3.

4.

E17–2   Debit   Credit

Calculation of deferred tax asset/liability: **End of 1998**   _____

E17–3   Debit   Credit

Calculation of deferred tax asset/liability: **End of 1998**   _____

E17–4   Debit   Credit

Calculation of deferred tax asset/liability: **End of 1998**   _____

E17–5   Debit   Credit

Calculation of deferred tax asset/liability: **End of 1998**   _____   _____

E17–6 or E17–7   **Debit**   **Credit**

    12/31/98:

    Calculation of deferred tax asset/liability (end of 1998):   **End of 1998** _____

    12/31/99:   **Debit**   **Credit**

    Calculation of deferred tax asset/liability (end of 1999):   **End of 1999** _____

    12/31/00:   **Debit**   **Credit**

E17–8 or E17–9

E17–10   **Debit**   **Credit**

    Calculation of deferred tax asset/liability: **End of 1998** _____

E17–11 or E17–12   Debit   Credit

Calculation of deferred tax asset/liability: **End of 1998** _____ _____

E17–13 or E17–14   Debit   Credit

Calculation of deferred tax asset/liability: **End of 1998** _____ _____

E17–15

E17–16   Debit   Credit

Income tax refund receivable calculation:

Calculation of deferred tax asset/liability: **End of 2000**   _____   _____

E17–17 or E17–18   Debit   Credit

Calculations:

E17–19

E17–20

	Current	Noncurrent

E17–21

Trevino Company

Partial Income Statement

For the Year Ended December 31, 1998

Income from the continuing operations before taxes	

E17–22

1.

Trevino Company

Partial Income Statement

For the Year Ended December 31, 1998

2.

P17–1

	Debit	Credit

Taxable income:

Calculation of deferred tax asset/liability: **End of 1998** _____

P17–2 or P17–3

Schedule of Temporary Differences

	1997	1998	1999	2000

1. Journal entry at end of 1997:

	Debit	Credit

Calculation of deferred tax asset/liability (end of 1997):   **End of 1997** _____

P17–2 or P17–3 (concluded)

2. Journal entry at end of 1998:   **Debit**   **Credit**

Calculation of deferred tax asset/liability (end of 1998):   **End of 1998** _____

Journal entry at end of 1999:   **Debit**   **Credit**

Calculation of deferred tax asset/liability (end of 1999):   **End of 1999** _____

Journal entry at end of 2000:   **Debit**   **Credit**

Calculation of deferred tax asset/liability (end of 2000):   **End of 2000** _____

P17–4 or P17–5

Journal entry at end of 1998:   **Debit**   **Credit**

Taxable income:

Calculation of deferred tax asset/liability (end of 1998):   **End of 1998** _____ _____

Journal entry at end of 1999:   **Debit**   **Credit**

Taxable income:

Calculation of deferred tax asset/liability (end of 1999):   **End of 1999** _____ _____

Journal entry at end of 2000:   **Debit**   **Credit**

P17–4 or P17–5 (concluded)

Taxable income:

Calculation of deferred tax asset/liability (end of 2000):

P17–6

1.

Calculation of deferred tax asset/liability:

2.

P17–7	Book		Tax	
Depreciation schedules:				
1998				
1999				
2000				
2001				
2002				
Annually, next 15 years				

P17–7 (concluded)

Calculation of deferred gain on sale of land in 1999:

Calculation of deferred tax asset/liability (end of 1999):   **End of 1999**   _____   _____

Calculation of deferred tax asset/liability (end of 2000):   **End of 2000**   _____   _____

Calculation of deferred tax asset/liability (end of 2001):   **End of 2001**   _____   _____

P17–8	1998	1999	2000	Later Years
1. Pretax financial income:				

Taxable income:

2. Journal entry at end of 1998:   **Debit**   **Credit**

Calculation of deferred tax asset/liability (end of 1998):   **End of 1998** _____ _____

Journal entry at end of 1999:   **Debit**   **Credit**

Calculation of deferred tax asset/liability (end of 1999):   **End of 1999** _____

P17–8 (concluded)

2. cont.   Journal entry at end of 2000:   Debit   Credit

Calculation of deferred tax asset/liability (end of 2000):   End of 2000 _____

3.   Debit   Credit

P17–9 or P17–10

Journal entry at end of 1998:   Debit   Credit

Taxable income:

Calculation of deferred tax asset/liability: End of 1998 _____ _____

P17–11

Journal entry at end of 1999:   Debit   Credit

Calculation of deferred tax asset/liability:

P17–12

1.

	1997	1998	1999

2. Journal entry at end of 1997:

	Debit	Credit

Calculation of deferred tax asset/liability (end of 1997):

P17–12 (concluded)

2. cont.   Journal entry at end of 1998:   **Debit**   **Credit**

Calculation of deferred tax asset/liability (end of 1998):

Journal entry at end of 1999:   **Debit**   **Credit**

Calculation of deferred tax asset/liability (end of 1999):

E18–1 or E18–2 | Debit | Credit

a)

b)

c)

E18–3 or E18–5 | Debit | Credit

E18–4 or E18–6 | Debit | Credit

1.

E18-4 or E18-6 (concluded) | Debit | Credit

2.

E18-7

Year	Ending Market Price	Option Price	Compensation Per Share	Aggregate	Accrued Percentage	Comp. Accrued to Date	Expense 1997	1998	1999
1997									
1998									
1999									

Debit | Credit

E18-8 | Debit | Credit

1.

E18–8 (concluded)	Debit	Credit
2.		

E18–9 or E18–10	Debit	Credit
1.		
2.		

E18–12	Debit	Credit
1. 1/15:		
1/20:		

E18–12 (concluded)   Debit   Credit

  1. 2/10:

      3/1:

      4/15:

      12/31:

  2.

E18–13 or E18–14   Debit   Credit

E18–16   Debit   Credit

  1. a)

E18–16 (concluded) | | Debit | Credit

1. b)

   c)

   d)

2. | | Common Stock | Contrib. Capital in Excess of Par | Retained Earnings | Total

   a)

   b)

   c)

   d)

E18–17 | Par Value: | $100,000 | $500,000 | $600,000
| | Preferred | Common | Total

Fraction of total par value:

1.

2.

3.

Instructor _____ Section _____ Name _____

E18–17 (concluded)	Par Value	$100,000	$500,000	$600,000
		Preferred	Common	Total

4.

5.

E18–18		Preferred	Common

E18–19		Debit	Credit
a)			
b)			
c)			
d)			

E18–19 (concluded)   Debit   Credit

e)

f)

g)

h)

E18–20

Item	Assets	Liabilities	Capital Stock	Other Contributed Capital	Retained Earnings
			Stockholders' Equity		
1.					
2.					
3.					
4.					
5.					
6.					
7.					
8.					
9.					
10.					
11.					
12.					
13.					
14.					
15.					
16.					
17.					
18.					
19.					
20.					

E18–22

Retained earnings, December 31, 1998				$	9 0 0 0 0 0	

E18–23

	Debit	Credit
1. a)		
b)		
c)		
d)		
2.		

E18–24

	Debit	Credit
1. a)		
b)		

E18–24 (concluded)	Debit	Credit
c)		
d)		
e)		
f)		
g)		
h)		
i)		

2.

Manning Lumber Company

Balance Sheet

(immediately after quasi-reorganization)

Assets		Liabilities and Stockholders' Equity	

P18–1 or P18–2	Debit	Credit

P18–3

Lanin Company

Statement of Stockholders' Equity

December 31, 1998

Contributed capital:

P18–4

	Capital Stock		Contrib. Captial	Retained
December 31, 1997:	Shares	Amount	in Excess of Par	Earnings

	Capital Stock		Contrib. Capital	Retained	
December 31, 1998:					

	Capital Stock		Contrib. Capital	Retained	Treasury Stock	
December 31, 1999:	Shares	Amount	in Excess of Par	Earnings	Shares	Amount

P18-5

Year	Ending Market Price	Option Price	Compensation Per Share	Compensation Aggregate	Accrued Percentage	Compensation Accrued to Date	Compensation Expense				
							1998	1999	2000	2001	2002
1998											
1999											
2000											
2001											
2002											

Journal Entries:

12/31/98:

	Debit	Credit

12/31/99:

12/31/00:

12/31/01:

	Debit	Credit

12/31/02:

P18–6 or P18–7	Debit	Credit
1. a)		
b)		
c)		
d)		

2.

Raabe Corporation

Statement of Stockholders' Equity

December 31, 1998

P18–8	Debit	Credit
1. a)		
b)		

P18–8 (continued)

	Debit	Credit
1. c)		
d)		
e)		

2.

Lopez Company

Statement of Stockholders' Equity

December 31, 1998

	Debit	Credit
3.		
a)		
b)		

P18–8 (concluded)

3. cont.	Debit	Credit
c)		
d)		
e)		

4.

Lopez Company

Statement of Stockholders' Equity

December 31, 1998

P18–9

Kent Corporation

Statement of Stockholders' Equity

December 31, 1999

P18–10 or P18–11 Journal Entries	Debit	Credit

P18–10 (concluded)

2.

P18–11 (concluded)

	Alternative				
	a)	b)	c)	d)	e)

	Alternative				
	f)	g)	h)	i)	j)

P18–12

	Year	Net Income
Calculation of retained earnings available for dividends at December 1998:	1994	
	1995	
	1996	
	1997	
	1998	
	Total	

Calculation of distribution:

	4% Preferred $100,000	7% Preferred $1,000,000	Common $500,000	Total

P18–13

1.

King Corportaion

Statement of Changes in Retained Earnings

Year Ended December 31, 1998

2.

P18-14

	Preferred Stock	Common Stock	Cont. Capital in Excess of Par	Other Cont. Capital	Treasury Stock	Retained Earnings Appr.	Retained Earnings Unappr.	Total
Dec. 31, 98								

P18–15

Year	Stock	1. Cumulative and Fully Participating	2. Noncumulative and Fully Participating	3. Cumulative and Nonparticipating	4. Noncumulative and Nonparticipating
1999	Preferred				
	Common				
2000	Preferred				
	Common				
2001	Preferred				
	Common				
2002	Preferred				
	Common				
2003	Preferred				
	Common				

Calculations:

P18–16

Pinder Corporation
Stockholders' Equity
December 31, 1998

Calculations:

P18–17   Beck Company

Stockholders' Equity

June 30, 1999

Notes:

P18–18

1. a)	f)
b)	g)
c)	h)
d)	i)
e)	j)

2.	Martin Corporation

Statement of Retained Earnings

End of Current Year

P18–18 (concluded)

3.   Martin Corporation

                        Stockholders' Equity Section of Balance Sheet

                                    End of Current Year

P18–20

	Debit	Credit
1.		
2.		

E19–1 or E19–3

1.

2.

	Debit	Credit

Calculations:

3.

	1998	1997	1996	1995	1994

E19–2

1.

2.

	Debit	Credit

Calculations:

3.

E19–4

Net Income (Including Cumulative Effects If Applicable)

	1998	1997	1996
1. FIFO to average cost			
2. LIFO to FIFO			

E19–5

	Debit	Credit
1. a)		
b)		

2.	1998	1997

3.	1998	1997

E19–6

Situation A:

1.

2.	Debit	Credit

3.

Situation B:

1.

2.	Debit	Credit

E19–6 (concluded)

Situation B (concluded):

3. _____

Situation C:

1. _____

2. _____

	Debit	Credit

3. _____

4. _____

E19–7 or E19–8

	Debit	Credit

E19–9

Item	Total Revenue	Total Expense	Total Assets	Total Liabilities	Owners' Equity
a)					
b)					
c)					
d)					
e)					

U = Understatement

O = Overstatement

N = No effect

E19–10

Item	97 Income	98 Income	Entry at December 31, 1998
a.			
b.			
c.			
d.			
e.			
f.			

E19–11

	1997 Statements			1998 Statements		
Item	Cost of Goods Sold	Total Assets	Net Income	Cost of Goods Sold	Total Assets	Net Income
a.						
b.						
c.						

U = Understatement

O = Overstatement

N = No effect

E19–12

1.	Net Income		Total Assets December 31		Total Liabilities December 31	
	1997	1998	1997	1998	1997	1998
a)						
b)						
c)						
d)						

U = Understatement

O = Overstatement

N = No effect

E19–12 (concluded)

	Debit	Credit
2. a)		
b)		
c)		
d)		

E19–13 or E19–14

	Debit	Credit

2. (E19–14 only)

	1999 Corrected	1998 Corrected

E19–15

Item	1998 Income Statement			Balance Sheet, 12/31/98		
	Net Income	Cost of Goods Sold	Other Expense	Assets	Liabilities	Owners' Equity
b.						
c.						
d.						
e.						
f.						
g.						

P19–1

1. a)

Debit   Credit

Calculations:

b)

Debit   Credit

Calculations:	Year	DDB	Straightline	Difference
	1995			
	1996			
	1997			

c)

Debit   Credit

P19–1 (concluded)

1. c) Calculations:

2.

Southern Railway Corporation

Income Statement

For the Year Ending December 31, 1998

Leasing revenues

P19–2

	1998	1997	1996

P19–3

	Debit	Credit
1.		

Calculations:	Year:	Compl. Contract	Percent of Compl.	Difference
	Before 1996			
	1996			
	1997			
	Total			

P19–3 (concluded)

2.

Income Statement

	1998	1997	1996
Income before taxes			
Income tax expense			
Net income			

Statement of Retained Earnings

	1998	1997	1996
Beginning retained earnings, previous			

P19–4 or P19–5

P19–4 or P19–5 (concluded)

P19-6

1. Income statement:	12/31/94	12/31/95	12/31/96	12/31/97	12/31/98
Sales					
Beg. inventory					
Purchases					
Goods available					
Ending inventory					
COGS					
Gross margin					
Oper. expenses					
Net income					
Balance sheet:					
Current assets					
Total assets					
Current liabilities					
Total liabilities					
Stockholders' Eq.					

2.	Debit	Credit	

P19–7

1. Calculations:

2.   Debit   Credit

3. Income Statement: 1998   1997   1996

   Retained Earnings:

P19–8   Unadjusted   Debit   Credit   Adjusted

Balance sheet

P19–8 (concluded)

Income Statement	Unadjusted	Debit	Credit	Corrected

P19–9 is on the next page

P19–10

	Debit	Credit
1. a)		
b)		
c)		
d)		
e)		

continued on page 19–13

P19-9

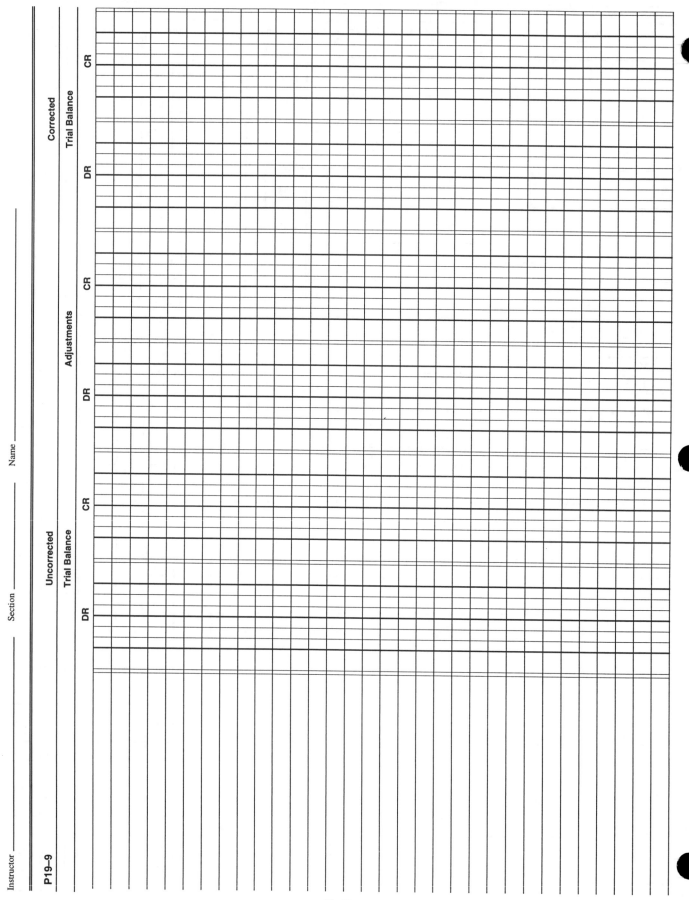

Uncorrected Trial Balance — DR — CR

Adjustments — DR — CR

Corrected Trial Balance — DR — CR

P19–10 (concluded)	Debit	Credit
1. f)		
g)		
h)		
i)		
j)		

2.		1998		1997	
Reported net income	$	240000	$	200000	

P19–11

	1996	1997	1998
1. Net income			

2.

	Debit	Credit

P19–12

Situation a calculations:

Situation b calculations:

P19-12 (concluded)

Bakker Construction Company

Condensed Statements of Income and Retained Earnings

For the Years Ended December 31, 1998 and 1997

	Situation A			Situation B			Situation C	
	1998	1997		1998	1997		1998	1997

	Situation C		
	1996	1997	1998

Situation c calculations:

P19–13 or P19–15   Debit   Credit

Entries:

---

2.   Traugh Company

Comparative Income Statements

For the years ending December 31,	1998	1997	1996

P19–13 or P19–15 (concluded)

	1998	1997	1996

2. (continued)

3. Accompanying footnotes:

P19–14

Correcting Entry at

	1996	1997	1998	December 31, 1998	
a)					
b)					
c)					
d)					
e)					
f)					
g)					
h)					
i)					

E20–1 or E20–3

Calculation of weighted average number of shares:

Shares	Weighting Factor	Weighted Shares

E20–2

a) For the quarter ended March 31, 1998:

Period of Time	Shares	Weighting Factor	Weighted Shares

b) For the six months ended June 30, 1998:

Period of Time	Shares	Weighting Factor	Weighted Shares

c) For the year ended December 31, 1998:

Period of Time	Shares	Weighting Factor	Weighted Shares

E20–4 or E20–5

Calculation of weighted average number of shares:

Shares	Weighting Factor	Weighted Shares

E20-6

Calculation of weighted average number of shares:

Shares	Weighting Factor	Weighted Shares

E20–7 or E20–8

Number of shares to be used in calculating BEPS:

Shares	Weighting Factor	Weighted Shares

Number of shares to be used in calculating DEPS:

Shares	Weighting Factor	Weighted Shares

E20–9 or E20–10

Calculation of weighted average number of shares:

Shares and Share Equivalents	Weighting Factor	Weighted Shares

BEPS: **DEPS:**

E20–12

Calculation of incremental shares for the options and warrants:

Series II warrants: DEPS

Series III warrants:

Series A options:

E20–12 (concluded)   DEPS

Series B options:

E20–13   BEPS   DEPS

1.

2. BEPS =

DEPS =

E20–14   DEPS

E20–15 or E20–16   BEPS   DEPS

E20–17   BEPS   DEPS

E20–18 or E20–19   BEPS   DEPS

  1. BEPS:

     DEPS:

  2. BEPS:

     DEPS:

  3. **(E20–19 only)**

E20–20   BEPS   DEPS

P20–1

1.

Milton Company

Stockholders' Equity Section of the Balance Sheet

December 31, 1998

Notes to financial statements:

2.

Instructor ________________ Section ________________ Name ________________

P20–2 or P20–3

1. BEPS:

2. DEPS:

P20–4

BEPS:

DEPS:

P20–5 or P20–6

1. BEPS:

2. DEPS:

P20–7

	Year	Calculations	Corrected EPS
1.	1994		
	1995		
	1996		
	1997		
	1998		

	Year	Calculations	Comparative EPS
2.	1994		
	1995		
	1996		
	1997		
	1998		

3. _____

P20–8

1. BEPS:

2. DEPS:

P20–9

1. Calculation of IPICSE of potentially dilutive securities:

Series I bonds:

Series II bonds:

Series III bonds:

Class A preferred stock:

Class B preferred stock:

Order:

2. BEPS:

DEPS:

P20–10

1. a) Convertible preferred stock:

P20–10 (concluded)

1. cont. b) 8 percent convertible bonds:

      c) 13 percent convertible bonds:

      d) 7 percent convertible bonds:

      e) stock options:

2. BEPS:

    DEPS:

E21–1

E21-2

James Company

Income Statement

For the Year Ended January 31, 1998

E21–3

	Beginning Balances		Ending Balances	

E21-4 or E21-5

E21-6

Quaker Company

Balance Sheet

December 31, 1998

Assets

Liabilities and Owners' Equity

E21-7

a)

b)

c)

d)

E21–7 (concluded)

e)

f)

E21–8

	Income Effect	Cash Effect	Activity
a)			
b)			
c)			
d)			
e)			
f)			
g)			
h)			
i)			
j)			
k)			
l)			
m)			
n)			
o)			

E21–10

	March 31	June 30	Sept. 30	Dec. 31
1. Property taxes				
2. Major repairs				
3. Inventory loss				

E21–11

E21–12	Ind. Parts	Small Engines
1.		

2. a)

b)

P21–1	Lilley Corporation
	Balance Sheet
	December 31, 1998

Assets

Liabilities and Equity

P21–2	Income Flows	Adjustments	Cash Flows
1.			

Horizon Corporation

Statement of Cash Flows

For the Year Ending December 31, 1998

P21–2 (concluded)

Reconciliation of net income to net cash provided by operations:

P21–3

Harley Manufacturing Company

Statement of Cash Flows

For the Year Ending December 31, 1998

P21–3 (concluded)

Reconciliation of net income (loss) to net cash provided by operating activities:

P21–4

	Income Flows	Adjustments	Cash Flows
1.			

2.

P21–5 or P21–6

Corporation

Worksheet for the Statement of Cash Flows

For the Year Ended December 31, 1998

	December 31, 1997	Analysis of Transactions DR	Analysis of Transactions CR	December 31, 1998

P21–7

Klawson Corporation

Statement of Cash Flows

For the Year Ended December 31, 1998

P21–8

Smith Corporation

Statement of Cash Flows

For the Year Ended December 31, 1998

P21–9

1. $ _____

2. $ _____

3. $ _____

4. $ _____

5. $ _____

6. $ _____

7. $ _____

8. $ _____

P21–9 (concluded)

9. $ _____

10. $ _____

11. $ _____

12. $ _____

13. $ _____

P21–11

Eller Company

Income Statement

For the Quarter Ended June 30, 1998

(in thousands of dollars)

EA–1

Item	Concept	Table
a)		
b)		
c)		
d)		
e)		

Item	Concept	Table
f)		
g)		
h)		
i)		
j)		

EA–2

1.
2.
3.
4.
5.
6.
7.

EA–3

1. a)
   b)
   c)
2. a)
   b)
   c)

EA–4

1. a)
   b)
   c)
2. a)
   b)
   c)
3. a)
   b)
   c)
4. a)
   b)
   c)

EA–5

1.
2.
3.
4.
5.

EA–6

1. _____
2. _____
3. _____
4. _____
5. _____
6. _____

EA–7

EA–8

EA–9

1. _____

2. Time line: ⟵ _____ ⟶

EA–10

Market Rate of Interest

	1.	4%	2.	10%

EA–11

Time line: ⟵ _____ ⟶

EA–12	Item	Concept	Calculations	Answer
	1.			
	2.			
	3.			
	4.			
	5.			
	6.			

EA–13

1. Time line: ⟵ ⟶

Year	Interest	Withdrawal	Balance
1			
2			
3			
4			

2. Time line: ⟵ ⟶

End of Year	Deposit	Interest	Balance
1			
2			
3			

3. Time line: ⟵ ⟶

EA–13 (concluded)

3. (continued)

Year	Interest	Withdrawal	Balance
1			
2			
3			

EA–14

Time line: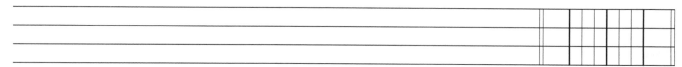

EA–15

Time line:

EA–16

Time line:

EA–17

Time line:

EA–18

Time line:

EA–19

Time line: $\longleftrightarrow$

1.

2.

EA–20

Time line: $\longleftrightarrow$

EA–21

Time line: $\longleftrightarrow$

EA–22

Time line: $\longleftrightarrow$

1.

2.

3.

EA–23

Time line: $\longleftrightarrow$

EA–24

Time line:

EA–25

Time line:

1.

2.

EA–26

Time line:

EA–27

Time line:

EA–28

Time line:

1.

EA–28 (concluded)

2.

Year	Beginning Investment	Interest	Cash Flow	Ending Investment
1				
2				
3				
4				
5				
6				

EA–29

Time line: ⟵ ⟶

PA–1

Time line: ⟵ ⟶

PA–2

Time line: ⟵ ⟶

PA–3

Time line: ⟵ ⟶

1.

2.

3.

PA–4

Time line:

1.

2.

3.

PA–5

Time line:

PA–6

	Year	Interest	Payment	Balance
	1			
	2			
	3			
	4			
	5			
	6			
	7			
	8			

PA–7

Time line:

PA–8

Time line:

Instructor _____ Section _____ Name _____

PA–9

Time line: ⟵————————————————————⟶

1. (a)

  (b)

2.

3. Earnings on the asset:

Year	Beginning Investment	Interest @ 12%	Cash Flows	Ending Investment
1				
2				
3				

Interest expense on the note:

Year	Beginning Liability	Interest @ 8%	Cash Flows	Ending Liability
1				
2				
3				

Year	Revenue	Interest Expense	Annual Net Income
1			
2			
3			

4.

PA–10

Time line: ⟵————————————————————⟶

1.

Year	Beginning Investment	+	Interest	+	Cash Flow	=	Ending Investment
1							
2							
3							
4							
5							
6							

PA–11

Time line: $\longleftarrow \longrightarrow$

1.

2.

3.

| | Debit | Credit |

PA–12

Time line: $\longleftarrow \longrightarrow$

1.

2.

Year	Beginning Investment	+	Interest	=	Ending Investment
Jan. 1, 1998					
Dec. 31, 1998					
Dec. 31, 1999					
Dec. 31, 2000					
Dec. 31, 2001					
Dec. 31, 2002					
Dec. 31, 2003					
Dec. 31, 2004					
Dec. 31, 2005					

PA–13

Time line: ←———→

1.

2.

PA–14

1. Time line: ←———→

2. Time line: ←———→

3. Time line: ←———→

4. Time line: ←———→

5. Time line: ←———→

6. Time line: ←———→

PA–15

1.

Bank	Calculation	Interest Rate
ONEOK Trust		
Mercantile Trust		
Farmer's National		
J. James State		

2.

Bank	Calculation	Investment
ONEOK Trust		
Mercantile Trust		
Farmer's National		
J. James State		
	Total	

3.

4. Time line: ←———————————————————————————→

PA–16

1. Time line: ←———————————————————————————→

2. Time line: ←———————————————————————————→

PA–16 (concluded)	Year	Interest	Payment	Balance
3.				
	1			
	2			
	3			
	4			
	5			
	6			
	7			
	8			
	9			

PA–17

   1. Time line: ⟵————————————————————————⟶

   2. Time line: ⟵————————————————————————⟶

PA–18

   1. Time diagram: ⟵————————————————————————⟶

   2.

PA–19

1.

2.

	Year	Cash Flow	Interest	Ending Balance
	1			
	2			
	3			
	4			
	5			

PA–20

1.

2.

	Year	Beginning Balance	Interest	Ending Balance
	1			
	2			
	3			
	4			
	5			

PA–21

Payment on Dealer Loan:

Month	Beg. Balance	Interest	Payment	Ending Balance
1				
2				
3				
4				
5				
6				
7				
8				

Payment on Local Bank Loan:

PA–21 (concluded)

Month	Beg. Balance	Interest	Payment	Ending Balance
1				
2				
3				
4				
5				
6				
7				
8				

Payment on Credit Union Loan:

Month	Beg. Balance	Interest	Payment	Ending Balance
1				
2				
3				
4				
5				
6				
7				
8				

PA–22

1.

Year	Cash Flows	Factor	Present Value
1			
2			
3			

2.

Year	1	2	3	Total
1				
2				
3				

3.

	1	2	3
1			
2			
3			

PA–22 (concluded)

4.

	1	2	3

5.

	1	2	3	Total

6.

	1	2	3

7.

PA–23

Instructor ______________________

P3–15

Account	etained Earnings		Balance Sheet	
		CR	DR	CR